CHRISTIANITY AN EVOLUTION IN IGBO CULTURE

A STUDY OF ACHEBE'S NOVELS

DR A. HAZEL VERBINA

ISBN 979-888530501-3

Contents

Foreword

The preparation of this book has been interesting and more challenging I have worked hard to find authentic and relevant materials for this topic. The innermost secrets of Colonization and its effect on the religion of the Igbo tribe have really paved the way to a deeper analysis of the Igbo people and their whereabouts after the Evolution process of Christianity in their tribal worship.

In one full attempt towards religion and its perspectives towards tribal people and their religion I have brought to view all the posibilities of how Christianity was an evolution in Igbo culture .

CHAPTER ONE

Christianity an Evolution in Igbo Culture

"When the white man arrived, he had the Bible and we had the land; now, we have the Bible and he has the land." Archbishop Desmond Tutu.

"The white man is very clever. He came quietly and peaceably with his religion. We were amused at his foolishness and allowed him to stay. Now he has won over our brothers, and our clan can no longer act like one. He has put a knife on the things that held us together and we have fallen apart." — Chinua Achebe, *Things Fall Apart* (129) "Christianity is deeply entrenched in several African countries and has denigrated and replaced indigenous religions and belief systems, and in the process, negatively affected whatever is left of her civilization. Africans and their indigenous religious beliefs and practices were demonized" (Blake, 67).

As Gikandi observes, Christianity is the major force through which the Africans were alienated from their culture, home and clan, and the violence was quite excruciating. When Christianity is not represented as an agent of colonial domination and violence, it appears as the ambiguous force of civilization and Europeanization. Christianity and the Christian missions appear in society as mere pressures of modernization and Europeanization rather than salvation. "Direct European colonial control of the earth's surface grew in the nineteenth century to nearly percent in a period that coincided with the rapid expansion of European Christianity in the non-western world" (Cox, 4).

Gikandi observes that "The association of Christianity and Colonialism has been one of the most powerful themes of African Literature, it just one dimension in a complex history" (150). It was, however, during the age of European colonization in the nineteenth century that Christianity and Christian missions in African came to play a crucial part in the transformation of the culture of the continent, especially in those areas that were no longer under Islamic influence or within the spheres of influence of the old Christian communities. As the dominant European powers entered into the scramble for Africa, Christianity provided one of the most powerful ideological justifications for colonization and missionaries served as important agents in the partition of Africa into different zones of influence. (Gikandi, 151)

As observed by Gikandi, the civilization of Africa sprung from the missions. Christianity was not only the destiny of the missionaries but to have a 'social upliftment' as well as Christianity. Achebe has portrayed the real mission through the character of Mr Brown in *Things Fall Apart*. He begins a small school and walks from door to door inviting students. The foremost duty of the Christian Missionary was to civilize the people for which they chose education as a foundation. "Many Africans flocked to Christian missions because of the opportunities they provided within the economy of colonialism" (TFA, 153).

Gikandi states the two great effects of the Christian Mission. They are the mental colonization, and The arising of the individual church. When we take into consideration the ideas of Loomba and Gikandi is very luminous. Religion and civilization was a means of transport that the white man adopted to colonize the land. "In fact, religious conversion begins to figure as a justification for economic plunder" (Loomba, 99). Ania artistically portrays the mindset of the colonizers through the speech of an Indian Queen who 'celebrates her conversion to Christianity' (Loomba, 99). The speech of the queen states that she was very much aware of the plundering that she deliberately allowed, and all that was in exchange for the 'celestial knowledge.' (Loomba, 99) Furthermore in her speech, she puts emphasis on two major and sensitive spots. First is washing or civilizing the black into White that has been made facile through Christianity. The second is that plundering the colonial area is justified through the 'gift of Christianity' (99). The statement of washing the black literally means converting the native completely into the customs and the visions of the British Government. "Colonialism, we have seen, reshapes, often violently, physical territories, social terrains as well as human identities" (155). This book brings into focus the evolution that Christianity brings among the Igbo tribes. Igbo is one of the three major tribes of Nigeria, the other two being Hausa and the Yoruba. Most of the Hausa are Muslims and Yoruba are Christian as well. The Igbo were scattered throughout Nigeria and that is why they became victims of the power of Christianity. The majority of the Igbo people were Christians who belong to the south-eastern part of Nigeria.

The society of Umuofia, the village in *Things Fall Apart*, was totally disrupted by the coming of the European government, missionary Christianity, and so on. That was not a temporary disturbance; it was a once and for all alteration of their society. To give an example of Nigeria, where the novel is set, the Igbo people had organized themselves in small units, in small towns and villages, each self-governed. With the coming of the British, Igbo land as a whole was incorporated into a totally different polity, to be called Nigeria, with a whole lot of other people with whom the Igbo people had not had direct contact before. The result of that was not something from which one could recover. It focuses on the Igbo people who 'inhabit the territory of southeastern Nigeria' on either side of the River Niger. Achebe deliberately attempts to construct a variegated, unsentimental and empathetic image of Igbo life prior to their personal contact with white missionaries, English culture and imperialism" (Searle, 50). "The Igbo people share a common language (although there are different dialects in various regions) and common religious beliefs and practices. A number of anthropologists and commentators have asserted that they also worship a supreme deity, Chukwu the creator" (Salami, 15). "The Igbo Christianity was part of the long history of Christianity in Africa that had flourished in North Africa until Islam overran it in 8 the century" (Okuma, 70). Blake quotes Yulisa Amadu: "Western missionaries, in their earliest contacts with Africa, ventured into the interior of Africa, thereby coming sometimes face to face with African traditions and customary practices which they could not fathom or understand. They then found it useful to speak of the "savage heathen," and the less adventurous colonial administrators emphasized the same theme, adding the "dark continent" myth" (60). "Achebe scrupulously creates the sense of a rich and coherent social fabric that has formed its own ideas about whites and their culture: this operates as a crucial background informing the reception of the first white missionary amongst the Igbo people" (Searle, 51).

The white man arrived during Okonkwo's exile. He was called an Albino by the natives and the bicycle that he drove was called an iron horse.Obrieka informs Okonkwo about the arrival of the white man in Abame and their destruction. Even though it was warned by the oracle that the white man will come like locusts, the people of Abame were lethargic and thus came into their clutches. Obreika went to meet Okonkwo in exile once again after two years from his previous visit. By then "The Missionaries had come to Umuofia. They had built their churches there. Won a handful of converts and were already sending evangelists to the surrounding town and villages" (105). The purpose of Obrieka to visit Okonkwo was, Nwoye was found along with the missionaries and Obreika was shocked to see Nwoye with them that forced him to meet Okonkwo. Umuofia was already flocked with missionaries. "The arrival of the missionaries had caused a considerable stir in the village of Mbanta" (TFA, 105).

People in Mbanta came to see him, when he started to speak he said that he was one among them and he has been sent by the god himself to protect them from their evil ways. The white man said, "We have been sent by this great God to ask you to leave your wicked ways and the false gods and to turn to him so that you may be saved when you die" (TFA, 106). But the statement can be proved false because it is true that the missionaries did not arrive in the African land to save or to protect the people from the false gods,

"The attempt to create non-white Christian leaders for the Christian church was essential to the missionary aspiration to create a multiracial commonwealth of Christians within the setting of Britain's empire" (Cox, 17). That is the reason that the missionaries were very keen on converting the natives. The people were ignorant and yielded quickly to temptation just like Nwoye who was captivated by the logic of the trinity. "He did not understand it. The words of the hymn were like drops of frozen rain melting on the dry plate of the panting earth. Nwoye's callow mind was greatly puzzled" (TFA, 108).

Just like Nwoye the people of Mbanta was indeed attracted to the religion rather than to the Gospel. It was a sheer mistake of the clan to give a piece of land to the missionaries. Just as Cox quotes Archbishop Desmond Tutu saying "When the white man arrived, he had The Bible and we had the land; now, we have The Bible and he has the land" (4). The missionaries "asked for a plot of land to build their church" (109). The elders thought, by giving them a part of the evil forest they could be easily sent out of their clan. "They offered them as much of the Evil forest as they cared to take. And to their greatest amazement, the missionaries thanked them and burst into a song" (TFA, 109). The leaders of Mbanta were shocked indeed by their behaviour. They expected them to be dead within a day or two but in vain. They started building the church. This situation induced the people to believe that the white man had unbelievable power. The white man started having frequent converts from then on. To abandon the gods of one's father and go about with a lot of effeminate men clucking like old hens was the very depth of abomination. Okonkwo was greatly grieved when he came to know that his son Nwoye had left him to join the alien God. Certain beliefs of the clan were out ruled by the alien religion. This paved the way for the natives to believe and follow the religion. Nneka the wife of Amadi a prosperous farmer was sent out of the family because she gave birth to twins in her four previous pregnancies and the worst part of it is the twin babies were thrown in the evil forest considering it as an abomination of the society. Moreover, the church accepted even the Osu, and this created a great stir among the people of Mbanta and people started thinking maybe their religion is rather powerful. "Achebe talks of Christianity, the new religion which could capture the heart and minds of the Igbos. They accepted the new God as 'real' and 'supreme' (Pandey, 52).

Achebe brings to light the real impact of the arrival of Christianity in his novels. It was merely politics rather than civilizing and giving the Gospel to the people. In *Things Fall Apart* Achebe makes it very much obvious to us that the white man arrived in their land not only to deliver the people from their sins but also to bring his government along with him. "The white man had not only brought a religion but also a government. It was said that they built a place of judgment in Umuofia to protect the followers of their religion. It was even said that they hanged one man who killed a missionary." (TFA, 114). Gikandi states it very aptly that: Much more than the task of converting souls, Christianity was to become important in Africa—and attractive to Africans—because of its association with the ideology of progress and modernity, both in terms of the material life of Christian converts, who were the first to be admitted into the institutions of capitalism and Westernization as diverse as trading stations and schools, and in terms of its promotion of a new code of conduct often based on Victorian values. As a consequence of this association of Christianity and modern culture, some of the most influential Africans of the nineteenth and early twentieth centuries were converted to Christianity. (152) "The Igbo are religious people. This is to say that they carry their religion wherever they are, in the field of sowing seeds or harvesting the crops to ceremonies, parties, funerals and so on. It is this fact that makes the Igbo so religious. In fact, religion occupies their whole system of being" (Okuma, 69). It is this concept of religiousness that helps and makes it easy for the white man to establish his religion in the African land. "Achebe seems to be attempting to recapture and dramatize the contingent nature of, and possibilities inherent within, the historical moment of encounter between these two very different cultures and religions" (Searle, 52). "A continuum is established on the basis of their shared humanity, which prevents them from being completely alien to one another.

Nwoye had questions that could not be answered within the traditional framework of Igbo culture that was met by the ministry of the missionaries, concerning the brittleness of an unrelentingly masculine code of behaviour, the exposure of twins, the sacrifice of his beloved friend Ikemefuna, and a dry hunger in his soul" (52). After the entry of Christianity, many customs and beliefs followed by the Igbo people were altered. People did not accept the religion just because the missionaries told about the Trinity or about the supreme God. In fact, they witnessed proof of their well-being even after residing in the evil forest and also accepting the outcast into their church. Mr Brown was the first missionary to begin the Christian enterprise in the Igbo land. He was friendly, flexible and easily approachable through which he gained the hearts of many people. Though the people called him a mad man, many people started coming to his school to educate themselves. The jovial and flexible character of Mr Brown made it easy for Mr Kiaga to establish his church in Mbanta. As Alison observes "While Mr Brown was loosely affiliated to the distant imperial authorities, Mr Brown pre-eminently desired religious conversion; he was not interested in delivering 'Christian civilization' as an exclusive and uncompromising British product designed to subjugate and destroy the existing culture (TFA,53). Mr Brown wants to be a real Missionary rather than being an intruder amongst the people. "Achebe depicts the power of Christian mission which focused on breaking down community norms. The Christian mission aided the colonization process by pursuing a policy of aggression" (Pandey, 121). Mr.Kiaga insisted on the people to believe in the true God but not to destroy certain beliefs but it was the evolution of the natives themselves which led them astray from their religion and clan. For instance, the killing of the Royal Python which is called 'father' by the natives. It was Okoli's own idea to kill the python but the rage was towards the church and its disciplines. Mr Kiaga comes to know about this only after he came to know that "The village has outlawed them" (TFA, 118).

It was just the beginning of the transition. In the meanwhile, the people of Mbanta became less ferocious after the death of Okoli the same night he killed the Royal Python. "His death showed that the gods were still able to fight their own battles. The clan saw no reason then for molesting the Christians" (118). Mr Kiaga had a balanced relationship with the natives and also with their religion. Alison observers: Mr Kiaga staunchly opposed the prejudices of new converts against outsiders like the Osu and preserved the tenuous equilibrium of the group through his firm resistance to extreme acts against the traditional religion, such as killing the sacred royal python. This balance was shattered by the hard-line authoritative approach of the final representative missionary who came to replace Mr Brown. He fits the stereotype of the missionary as an arrogant imperial agent, often implicitly constructed by postcolonial discourse as the pre-eminent model of evangelistic endeavour. (53).

Christianity brought a great exodus in the custom and manners of the people. This religion posed a great threat to the life and tradition of the Igbo. Okonkwo was furious about the great exodus that religion has caused to his people and the clan. The religion did not remain in itself just converting the people who embraced 104 the religion but also caught the roots of the clan, for instance, the conversion of Ogbuefi Ugonna a man of two titles who was "the first man in Umuofia to receive the sacrament of the Holy Communion."(TFA, 217). It did not remain just with the conversion of the great leaders but also "They had built a court where the District Commissioner judged the case of ignorance." The white man has entered into the land as an evangelist to save the people from their paths of sin. Instead, he has come and has brought his religion and the government as well. Okonkwo's anger raged not towards the white man but toward his own people. "Okonkwo was deeply grieved. And it was not just a personal grief. He mourned for the clan, which he saw breaking up and falling apart and he mourned for the warlike Umuofia, who had so unaccountably become soft like women.

Christianity brought such profound changes in the clan that the people were so much carried away, and "The new religion and government and the trading stores were very much in the people's eyes and mind" (133), that they totally forgot about the return of Okonkwo the 'Roaring Falme' as he is popularly called. Ultimately, due to the arrival of the white man and his 'lunatic religion' many trading stores were built "and for the first time palm oil and kernel became things of great price, and much money flowed into Umuofia ' (130). People experienced a 'growing feeling' towards the religion since they found that the religion in no way affected the people but out of which the land was developed and the revenue was increasing. "This growing feeling was due to Mr Brown, the white missionary who was very firm in restraining his flock from provoking the wrath of the clan" (130).

Initially, when Christianity entered the land of Umuofia it was for the betterment and to civilize the people. This can be understood by the behaviour of Mr Brown towards the clan and the respect that he held towards the leaders of the clan. This lead Akunna to send "one of his sons to be taught the white man's knowledge in Mr Brown's school" (130). Mr Brown indulged in long talks with Akunna about his religion and Christianity; by doing so he learnt a big deal about their religion and concluded that "a frontal attack on it would not succeed. And so he built a school and a little hospital in Umofia" (132). Mr Brown stooped down to conquer. He begged the people to send their children to school for he said that the future world will have only space for educated people and if they fail they will have strangers from outside to rule them. This was the reason that people like Akunna sent their son to know the knowledge of the Whiteman. As said by Mr Brown in the native court "the DC was surrounded by strangers who spoke his tongue. Most of these strangers cane from the distant town of Umuru on the bank of the Great River where the white man first went" (132). The natives yielded to such kind of temptation. They not only accepted his religion but also believed that the white man's medicine had a great effect and produced quick results.

From the very beginning religion and education went hand in hand." When the changes were happening so rapidly, it was then Mr Brown fell ill and had to leave. Mr Brown's balance and the mutual understanding "was shattered by the hard-line authoritative approach of the final representative missionary Reverend James Smith who came to replace Mr Brown. He fits the stereotype of the missionary as an arrogant imperial agent, often implicitly constructed by postcolonial discourse as the pre-eminent model of evangelistic endeavour" (Searle, 53).

It was the arrival of Smith that brought the real rigidness, rules and regulations in the religion as well as the society. He differentiated as black and white. To him obeying his government was more important than the salvation of the clan. The situation and the mutual relationship between the natives and the missionaries did not remain as expected. Things became even worse when Enoch killed one of the ancestral spirits. This was the first time that Mr Smith was able to understand the ferociousness of the Igbo religion because the sound of "the Mother of Spirits wailing for her son" (TFA, 136) affected Mr Smith very much. The next day a group of Egwugwu came to the church and destroyed it into a plain ground In spite of Mr Smith protesting against them, Okonkwo and the whole village was relieved. They were not really aware of the danger that is to come in future. Cox defines the theory of civilization, commerce and Christianity in the view of Carey. According to Carey civilization would be made easier only through the gospel wherein they can reform the inner qualities of a person rather easily. When the inner transformation is wrought out, they can be easily yielded to follow the western civilization which in turn would bring what is called civilized commerce. In the end, the missionaries after framing certain enterprises such as schools, hospitals, trade centres, were short of revenue and this forced them to generate it from the natives and also from unpaid labour.

In *Things Fall Apart* when the leaders of Umuofia are arrested, the District Commissioner asks the natives to pay two hundred bags of cowries in order to release them. *In Arrow of God* Mr Wright proposes unpaid labour to the people of Umuaro, so as to save the revenue of the British Government. The real effect of colonization lay in the structuring and deforming of the culture and the habits of the natives. The District Commissioner calls all the leaders of Umuofia for a meeting. The demolition and the destruction started by threatening and ill-treating the leaders of the clan. They were quite unaware of the backdrop of the European Government; they came to know about it only through the words of the District Commissioner: We have brought a peaceful administration to you and your people so that you may be happy. If any man ill-treats you we shall come to rescue. But we will not allow you to ill-treat others. We have a court of law where we judge cases and administer justice just as it is done in my own country under a great queen. I have brought you here because you joined together to molest others , to burn people's houses and their place of worship. That must not happen in the dominion of our queen, the most powerful ruler in the world. I have decided that you will pay a fine of two hundred bags of cowries. You will be released as soon as you agree to this and undertake to collect that fine from your people. (TFA, 141-142) It was quite surprising to the leaders of Umuofia that they were totally under the clutches of the white Government.

The colonization brought such havoc not only in the society but also had a deep psychological effect over the people. The people 108 were not allowed to move around and take decisions freely. This we come to know when Mr. Smith asserts: "That must not happen in the dominion of our queen, the most powerful ruler in the world." The people were swayed by the new rules of the white Government. Ultimately when the people gathered in the market place the court messengers arrived to inform them that they cannot hold a public meeting without getting prior permission from the clan. And thus Okonkwo was enraged and killed one of the court messengers and feeling ashamed of being hanged by an alien government he commits suicide. At the end of *Things Fall Apart*, the African world has lost jurisprudence over political power, leaving only the religious power of the sacred realm. *Arrow of God* charts the erosion of that religious power and *No Longer at Ease* charts how the sacerdotal operates within the remains of kinship rules. Hence, in *Arrow of God*, the recurrent intimations of slavery appear in relation to the transformations—or translations—of sacrifice, the necessary legitimization of such transformations, as well as its explicit reference to the private sphere of kinship as the realm that confers the powers of transformation. (Osinubi, 39)

Achebe has witnessed himself the transition due to Christianity. "In Home and Exile, Achebe writes that his father was the first Christian convert in his village. He asserts that his parents were sometimes uncompromising in their Christian belief. But he even admits that it was his Christian parents who made him realize the significance of Africa's culture" (Pandey, 48). 109 "Africa became a tool of criticism in the hands of the missionaries. They basically wrote about the darker side of African society, and sometimes they even misinterpreted what they saw" (16).

Achebe also reflects Christianity which causes another cultural conflict, a spiritual conflict in the village via converts "Go and burn your mothers' genitals," said one of the priests. The men were seized and beaten until they streamed with blood" (qtd Pandey, 38). The theme of disintegration of the society that began in *Things Fall Apart* follows in the next volume of the trilogy *Arrow of God*. It can be noted that in *Things Fall Apart* Okonkwo is enraged with anger knowing that his son Nwoye has joined the Christians. So he sends him out of his Obi and also warns him never to step inside his Obi again. In *Arrow of God* the transition reaches the next level wherein the Chief Priest sends his son Oduche to learn the ways of the white man aspiring that it would be of great help to him in critical situations. In Achebe's future works and narratives of nationalism and post colonialism would be played out of the full import of this Christian conquest of the traditional African Rituals and religious beliefs as dramatized in both *Things Fall Apart* and *Arrow of God* in which literally , *Things Fall Apart* and the arrow of the Christian God pierces through the African rituals , government and traditions leading to a devalorization of communities , producing general instability and the African world no longer and perhaps never to be again in ease. (Rose, 63) "Ezeulu likes to think that Oduche is in the Christian community as an uninvolved observer. But the situation admits no such ambivalence. One is either serving the Christian God or the ancestral deity; he cannot owe allegiance to both at the same time. By sending his son to the missionary Ezeulu is inextricably compromised, whether he recognizes or admits it or not" (Soile, 288).

The colonial effect has brought a drastic change not only in the character of the natives but also in the character of the Europeans, so to say in the character of Captain WinterBottom. He has come to Nigeria fifteen years before, and initially he was not happy about anything but his rigidness towards his service, and "His strong belief in the value of the British mission in Africa was, strangely enough, strengthened during the Cameroon campaign of 1916 when he fought against the Germans, and also he would not now exchange the life for the comfort of Europe" (AOG, 31). The second generation of people who witnessed and experienced the effect of colonization are the people of Umuaro and Okperi. It is in this novel that Achebe portrays a colonized atmosphere wherein it is totally occupied by foreign colonial administrators. The white man and his religion have consummately occupied Umuaro and have started to build roads and developed trade and commerce. The 'Gome' sound of the Ogene was replaced by the 'Gome, Gome' sound of the church bell which brought a fear of future in the minds of Ezeulu. "At first he had thought that since the white man had come with great power and conquest, it was necessary that some people should learn the way of his deity. That was why he had agreed to send his son to learn the 111 new ritual" (43). As days went on 'the religion was like a leper' (43) and Ezeulu was quite aware of the disintegration that the religion was going to bring to his land. The oracle has already prophesied that 'the white man had come to take over the land and rule' (44) and Ezeulu knew that the oracle was true because many things that related to the arrival of white man assured him that they will take over the land its customs and its religion, and there will be no speck of tradition or culture of Igbo left. When Nwafo tells Ezeulu that the ringing of the bell says "Leave your Yam, leave your cocoyam and come to church." Ezeulu replies thoughtfully, "It is singing the song of extermination" (44). So Ezeulu Knew very well that the religion and its government will really destroy each and every bit of the tradition, and a very conspicuous situation that validates the point is that when Oduche tries to kill the royal python by hiding it in a box. This is a situation which tells us that the natives in spite of accepting the alien religion were trapped, and they were stumbling to get rid of their traditional rituals and their practices they were accustomed to. Oduche did choose himself to be a Christian, but it was his father Ezeulu who sent him to learn the ways of Christianity . Ezeulu persuades Oduche through his conversation and convinces him to go to the school. He says “The world is like a Mask dancing. If you want to see it well you do not stand in one place. My spirit tells me that those who do not befriend the white man today will be saying had we known tomorrow” (47). Ezeulu’s intention was not bad. He was confused and always in a dilemma. He thinks that by sending his son he could resist the transition of his land but in vain. He was the victim of the transition both in the beginning and the end.

The forefathers have always placed God and religion at the heart of their culture, values and life. More so the traditional Igbo family before the coming of the early white missionaries had sacred spots in their families –here household altars were set up for family prayers, offering and sacrifices. It was not surprising to see most Igbo accepting Christianity, in spite of the initial difficulties and cultural differences. (Okuma, 70) In Arrow of God the transition first begins from the Chief Priest of Ulu. Oduche protests initially to join the religion but later on he begins liking the religion and the knowledge of the white man. He gets impressed by Mr. Blackett, a West Indian missionary who is said to have more knowledge than the white man. Thus, Oduche was enlightened with the religion and its values. The Christian teachers not only taught the old religion but were sure to destroy their old customs and beliefs. The first step that Mr. Good country takes against the religion is to destroy the Royal Python which is considered an abomination in the Christian religion. He told the converts "If we are Christians, we must be ready to die for the faith", 'he said. "You must be ready to kill the python as the people of the rivers killed the iguana. You address the phython as a father. It is nothing but a snake, the snake that deceived our first mother, Eve. If you are afraid to kill it do not count yourself a Christian" (AOG, 48). But there was a covert from Umuaro named Moses Unachukwu, called the first Christian, who highly protested and told "the new teachers quite bluntly that the catechism asked the converts to kill the python, a beast full of ill omen. Was it for nothing that God put a curse on its head? Asked Moses to the new converts" (AOG, 48). He even recited the reason behind the tradition and custom of which stopped the native from killing the Royal Python. The Englishman stood as cunning as ever because he wanted to find a way out to take these people out of their track, and he said that it is mere foolishness and such kinds of stories will not be allowed in God's house. Highly inspired by the talk of Mr. Good Country, Oduche decided to kill the Royal Python.

The religion not only confused the native rituals but also had a high impact on the psychology of the people. Oduche is a solid example of the psychological imbalance. He is perplexed in a situation wherein to believe The Bible or his bearers. At the end he decides to kill the Royal Python without hurting it but suffocating it to death. Through this he thinks that he did not defy his religion and also heeded the customs of the new religion. "Ezeulu succeeds in assessing the general situation by sending his son to the mission school, but he does not, and in fact, could not, provide for the incalculable eventuality due to human nature - this time, Oduche's sacrilegious attempt to kill the sacred python of Idemili" (Soile, 287). According to Soile "Christian mission, by its very definition biblically, is a cross-cultural enterprise, and thus raises many matters that are of crucial concern to postcolonial literatures and theory. Most profoundly it confronts one with issues of truth and morality: how the universal claims of Christianity are to be applied to the particulars of a given culture and locality" (49). "The religious and the pragmatic, which had combined to form the unified world view of the Igbo and given depth, stability and dignity to their life were now being split into opposing poles and confusion was inevitable" (Nwoga, 31).

Colonization was the real purpose of teaching the natives salvation civilization, and in no way it can be justified. The factual truth behind the Christian Mission is brought about in *Arrow of God.* The road from Okperi to Umuaro was built by the PWD department headed by Mr. Wright. The memorandum sent by the Lieutenant-Governor states to impose the effective system of "indirect rule" (TFA, 57) and the memorandum continues:

To many colonial nations, native administration means government by white men. You are all aware that H.M.G. considers the policy as mistaken. In place of the alternative of governing directly through Administrative Officer, there is the other method of trying while we endeavor to purge the native system of its abuses to build a higher civilization upon the soundly rooted native stock that has its foundation in the hearts and minds of the people and therefore on which we can more easily build, moulding it and establishing it into lines consonant with modern ideas and higher standards , and yet all the time enlisting the real force of the spirit of the people, instead of killing all that out and trying to start afresh . We must not destroy the African atmosphere, the African mind, the whole foundation of the race. (AOG, 57)

So it was this idea that enabled Winter Bottom to choose Ezeulu as paramount chief. The indirect rule method was where the natives will feel comfortable and oblige to the notions of the colonizers. From the beginning, the white man had a perfect mission. The fight and the controversy of the clan made it hasty for the white man to spread the enterprise and his domain in the land. The white came there camouflaged like Christian Missionaries not to save the people but to trap them in their government. Just like Ezeulu said "The new religion was like a leper. Allow him a hand shake he wants to embrace" (AOG, 43).

It was so with the Christian missionaries. They came with salvation and now they are embracing the natives towards their civilization, their culture and their aspiration .Even the strongest and the great leader of the clan falls prey to their scheme. The Igbos were very innocent and they sometimes very easily yielded. It was not for Igbos that the British Government built roads but for themselves to develop their merchandise, because they in no way want to risk their life in this alien land. Achebe states that "They were as loyal as pet dogs" (AOG, 77). Jeffery Cox distinguishes the British mission into two. The first is the formal power of military rule, law and slavery of the British government. The second is the informal power of massive, religious and then the scholarly inequality of others. "The first led missionaries to organize people into settled communities where they could receive the ministries of Christian institutions, especially schools. The second led missionaries to gather churches of voluntary committed believers first of all, and then deal with the problems of institution building afterwards" (Cox, 14).

The informal power was optimum. It is that power which enabled the British missionaries to deduce the people more appropriately. By establishing a good rapport and support through the means of religion and church, the missionaries were able to understand the potentiality of the native people and it was easier for them to know what they needed. "The attempt to create non-white Christian leaders for the Christian church was essential to the missionary aspiration to create a multiracial commonwealth of Christians within the setting of Britain's empire" (15).

Achebe has fully wrought the action of colonization in his novel *Arrow of God.* As per the memorandum 'the indirect rule was implied' and thus many native teachers, officers and heads were appointed in order to make the errand of the British Government easier. The mission's another enterprise was slavery, and the utmost flight of slavery is encompassed in *Arrow of God.* Mr. Wright is the perfect embodiment of a British leader .He was not amicable, nor approachable .When he was appointed by the PWD to build the road to Umuaro, he urged to get rid of the situation by building the road fast and getting rid of that place. When given a suggestion to reduce the salary to the labourers to two pence for three pence he went even further to give the idea of free labour.

The colonial mentality was always awake in him and to him the road was built for the black and it is their duty to work for it. And thus he involved the natives by convincing them to help him build the road. The natives worked like slaves in their own country, unable to deduce what they are endangered with. It was then Obika was whipped by Mr. Wright for coming late to work. The people were so ignorant of the fact that they were constructing their own road towards slavery. The fight between the natives aggravates Mr. Wright and, enraged in anger he calls them as 'black monkeys' (AOG, 83). Subsequently there is a meeting arranged by the natives protesting that they would no longer work for the roads. They want to revolt against the white men, but Moses warns them by telling them that they are taking their own trouble in their hands. He also tells them "As daylight chases away darkness so will the white man drive away all our customs" (83). Achebe, through the words of Moses, reveals that it was mere colonization which has induced the white people to come to Africa. Moses says "The white man, the new religion, the soldiers, the new road – they are all part of the same thing. The white man has a gun, a matchet, a bow and carries fire in the mouth. He does not fight with one weapon alone" (86). Thus the natives were able to understand that they were completely in the clutches of the white man. Even the chief priest Ezeulu was in a dilemma whether to ask for an explanation or not. It is very much evident from this scene that the white man he does not have any distinction among the native people and to him all are black slaves through whom he can extract work. Achebe contrasts the French and the British colonization. According to him "The French made up their minds about what they wanted to do and did it.The British, on the other hand, never did anything without first sending out a Commission of Inquiry to discover all the facts, which then ham-strung them" (107).

Jeffery Cox observes that the rise and control of the European colonies and the rapid spread of the Christianity by the missionaries was a simultaneous process. The Colonial agents were in the disguise of Christian Missionaries. Clarke *in Arrow of God* really abuses the policy of the British both in the concept of the native chief as well as generating reports about them. To him British colonization is beating around the bush whereas the French Colonization hits the target. Gradually the attempt of conquering the land and the people is achieved by the British Government, as in *Arrow of God*. Through the words of Ezeulu and Moses we are very much aware that the British have duly occupied the land and their force is intact over the natives. Having experienced the peril and the motive of the white man's religion, personally Ezeulu refuses to become the paramount chief, because he does not want to be used as a weapon to destroy his own religion, just like Oduche who in the end is totally carried away by the whims and fancies of the religion, its personality, it aura and its knowledge. The truth that underlies why the native joined the white government is revealed through the words of John Nwodika's son. He said that it was the white man's money that brought him here and the sooner the better; he joined the group because he heard that the people from other clans were flocking to reach that place. He also clears the doubt that he is not a cook but the one who keeps things in order. Moreover he reveals that he did not want to die a servant. "My eye is on starting a small trade in tobacco as soon as I have collected little money. People from other places are gathering much wealth in this trade and in the trade of cloth" (171).

The threats of the British Government started with slavery and then appointing paramount chief so that they would smell each and every move of the natives and it would be easier for them to rule the country. As soon as Ezeulu refuses, Clark, enraged with anger, says "In that case he goes back to prison." The British Government was authoritative whether it is his land or the land of the colonizers. His rule is rule and those who do not abide by his rule will surely meet the consequences. "In the modern world, then, we can distinguish between colonization as the takeover of territory, appropriation of material resources, exploitation of labor and interference with political and cultural structures of another territory or nation, and imperialism as a global system" (Loomba, 11).

Eventually colonization means a process that leads to domination and control. According to Loomba, colonialism is not a force, power or domination from outside. It is a force within yielding to the external force. The yielding of the internal force is shown by Achebe through his conversation of Ezeulu. He said "We have shown the white man the way to our house and given him a stool to sit on. If we now want him to go away again we must either wait until he is tired of his visit or we must drive him away" (AOG, 133). The action of the colonial force was not easy to attack externally; it was the internal acceptance, which made it easier for the colonizers to enter in the disguise of Missionaries. The people of Umuaro have been very relentless in accepting the Christianity as well as the

British administration since day one and even the benefits rendered by the Government. Moreover, even the chief priest himself was enthralled by the knowledge and the skill of the white man, which even persuaded him to advise his son Oduche to not only learn the way of the white man but also to acquire all the skills just like him. So he insists his son Oduche "to learn and master this man's knowledge so much that if you are suddenly woken up from the sleep and asked what it is you will reply. You must learn it until you can write it with your left hand" (191).

Cox observes that the mission was preparing the platform for the promotion of wage labour and trading. Both the trading and the mission activities helped each other mutually. The British Government saw the crisis that was taking place in Umuaro and thought it was the right chance to take the people under their control. It was really wise on the part of Ezeulu to send his son to learn the ways of the Christian. But Oduche was not like Moses the most important Christian in Umuaro, who entered like an innocent being and later grew in such a way that he was able to protest if any false doctrines were preached to them. He was indeed a stumbling block for Mr.Good Country. He even wrote a petition on behalf of the priest of Idemili stating that if the Royal Python is not allowed to live in peace "they would regret the date they ever set foot on the soil of the clan" (216).

The result of the petition was very positive; the Lieutenant Governor had advised the bishops not to interfere in the matters related to python. This brought the view of Ezeulu, that it is necessary to have some men like Moses to deal with the white Government to be true. "As a result many people –some of them very important –began to send their children to school. Even Nwaka sent a son-the one who seemed the least likely among the children to become a good farmer" (217). As discussed earlier, the main motive of the Christian mission was colonization. Eventually there was a great crisis in Umuaro; the chief priest had not announced the New Yam Festival and Good country took it as a fruitful opportunity to trap the natives. So he announced the harvest festival on the second Sunday of November "the proceeds from which will go into the fund of building a place of worship more worthy of God and of Umuaro" (217). So he sends the message telling that the people can offer Yam to the living God and can proceed with the harvest. Not only that they can offer any crop, livestock, money or anything. Initially it was the custom of the Igbo to offer just one Yam and so the new member was confused to give the message to the people. It was Moses who interrupted and said "If Ulu who is a false God and ate one Yam, the living God who owns the whole world should be entitled to eat more than one" (218).

Thus the Christian mission started every step towards not only civilizing or taking the Igbo in the path of salvation, but also fulfilling their enterprise. It is very well understood that the people of Umuaro can be convinced only with the fear of God and it is at this point that the white man understood and through the platform of religion they were able to drive people to their side. Achebe's mastery as a novelist is unveiled in each character. He had assembled characters of the novel in such a way that each individual manifests the characteristics and the highlights of the particular era. When British imperial officials allowed missionaries to enter the open door, and act as private agents to promote the Christian religion among non-Christians, they were allowing missionaries to enter into social relationships at a time of massive inequality between westerners and non-westerners, inequality that was not by any means limited to superior firepower on the part of European imperial powers. British missionaries entered a world beyond the boundaries of Britain where the social and racial superiority of the people of Britain over nonwestern peoples was treated as axiomatic. (Cox, 12)

The mutability of the Igbo tribe is wrought in an intelligent way by Achebe, especially the beginning and the stand by the Christian religion is marked in his two novels *Things Fall Apart* and *Arrow of God.* At the end of *Arrow of God* the transition is very well experienced. The mission is accomplished. All those who supported or joined the new religion and the new government benefited. For example, the son of Nwodika's dream came true. He started a small trade on tobacco. The Christian harvest had more natives. "In this extremity many a man sent his son with the Yam or two to offer to the new religion and to bring back the promised immunity. Thereafter any Yam harvested in his fields was harvested in the name of the son" (AOG, 232). Achebe's depiction of mission is a salutary reminder of the choice demanded by convictions that are universal in scope, which missionaries sought to apply to particular cultures. More pertinently, he traces the tragic cultural implications of imperialism, without allowing the missionary enterprise to be dismissed as simply the cynical or deluded attempts of an imperialistic nation to find ideological justification for their will to power at a global level. (Searle, 51)

No Longer at Ease charts the third generation after colonization. The setting is now from Umuofia to Lagos. In this novel Achebe traces the complete exploit of the native religion, its beliefs and customs. Even the breaking of the Kola nut was in the name of Jesus Christ Amen. People were completely transformed and whenever there was a sad or special occasion prayer meetings were called. "Obi's experience in *No Longer at Ease* reveals the implications of this double meaning: the word of white power also portends black spiritual decay and death" (Roger, 166). According to Cox "The ultimate goal of the church was a nation of Christian believers who, after receiving the ministries of the church, would in the words of the Book of Common Prayer, hereafter live a godly, righteous and sober life" (24). Christianity has brought drastic changes in the social structure, customs, beliefs, rituals and practices of the native people. The modern culture that lay beneath religion attracted many people and also the opportunities offered by the British Government. "Christianity thus came to be represented as an ambivalent force in African society. It was admired as one of the most important forces in the modernization of Africa. This was especially the case in the field of education and literacy" (Gikandi, 153).

In *No Longer at Ease* Achebe has portrayed the thirst for by the native people. They have begun an organization in the name of Umuofia Progressive Union so as to sponsor the young men who go abroad for education. "They have taxed themselves mercilessly". (NLE-6). The religion has brought education and modernity through which the natives were attracted, and that is represented in a very transparent way in *No Longer at Ease.* The effect of post colonialism is felt in every segment in the novel *No Longer at Ease.* The rise of individual churches and of the native pastor can be best illustrated through the character Reverend Samuel Ikedi and his St. Mark's Anglican Church. African Christians naturally appropriated aspects of Christianity that were useful to them and neglected aspects that were not, but the relationship between missionary and

African catechists, Bible women and congregation was often one of mutual respect and admiration, and cooperation in the pursuit of mutually agreed upon goals that were understood in the light of a common understanding of the meaning of Christianity." (Cox, 251)

The flourishing of Christianity brought changes in the internal as well as the societal affairs. For example, Pastor Ikedi gave the references of how wedding customs were totally declining and wedding passes were given in the form of invitations, which allowed the guest to participate in the wedding. He also makes the congregation clear that Umuofia in the past had the curse of blood on it and it is now delivered and the sin and curse had been washed by the Lamb of God. According to Cox, education had been central to the building of Christian institutions since the first days of the missionary movement in the eighteenth century, and missionary wives began schools for girls as part of their natural and normal role as a missionary wife (201). Christian growth in Africa often originated in medical and educational institutions. The great evangelical East African Revival that began in the 1930s spread from mission hospitals through its leaders Simeon Nsibambi and the CMS missionary doctor Joe Church. From a family of evangelical clergymen and missionaries, Church was searching for a higher spiritual life under the influence of the Keswick Convention when he met Nsibambi, a graduate of Anglican schools and government health officer." (Cox, 251)

Achebe has represented Africa in all its stages from its roots and its advancement in society and in political systems in his first novel. It can be very well understood that religion was the base of colonization. The Community Secondary Society was one of the most active missions in Umuofia. It was in that school that Obi Okonkwo was educated. Achebe brings to our view the evolution that it has brought about in every step of the tradition, especially in breaking of Kola nut. Many congregations of Christians entered into Africa, one among them was the Evangelist who was strictly against idol worship.

The third stage of Christianity is represented in *No Longer at Ease*. It is the post-colonial Nigeria we are witnessing that the Igbo people have completely transformed and there are just one or two left who have passion for the native tradition. For instance, when Obi leaves for London for his higher studies there is a meeting called for and the guests bless Obi with gifts. It is a custom to break kola nuts for any special occasion. Obi's father is not against the tradition of breaking the kolas nut but against the custom of offering it to the idols. He said to the guests "What I say is that it will not be used as a heathen sacrifice in my house" (NLE, 41). The Igbo tradition is entwined with the Christian practices; the kola nut is broken in the name of Jesus Christ. A man in Umuofia was judged by the titles, barns and the number of wives, but after colonization and the arrival of Christian Missionary, the custom of polygamy was considered a sin, and so the coverts got married only once. Obi is the grandson of Okonkwo of *Things Fall Apart*.

The transition that Christianity brought is felt in the three generations, Okonkwo, Nwoye and Obi Okonkwo. Okonkwo was a man of culture, tradition and customs. Nwoye his son is a staunch Christian convert. Obi Okonkwo, a young man of the postcolonial era exploited and immersed in the sea of modernization. Obi felt great whenever he heard about his grandfather. Many great men were born in his land and their greatness is unquestionable.

During the pos- colonization "Tiles are no longer great, neither are barns with a large number of wives and children. Greatness is now in the things of the white man. And so we too have changed our tune" (NLE, 43). The transition of black into white means a man plunging deep into religion. The former statement is true of the experiences that Obi has throughout the novel *No Longer at Ease*. The foremost duty of the mission enterprise was to wash away the sins of the black and lead them towards salvation. The black got civilized, educated and held government jobs but very easily yielded to the blackness of corruption .However the Mission failed to produce good individuals for the society. In *No Longer at Ease* the first half of the story is about the success of the mission wherein Obi Okonkwo has passed the Cambridge School Certificate, and is now eligible for a civil service job. The second half brings to our view the fall of Obi's tradition, religion, values and culture. It can be seen that the danger of the mission was not by the mission itself but by its influence over the people, especially related to the social practices.

Achebe's notion is to present before us the real devastation caused by religion and its practices and the hero and his family's response towards it. The Christian Mission did support the native pastors financially, but many taxes were levied in the form of class fees and other contributions. Apart from that, the native pastors have to pay the school fees as well as the church fees. Achebe has wrought the transition when Okonkwo the father of Isaac Okonkwo, was a man of title and had a huge compound in which his Obi was built, had three wives and his barn was full with yams. Nevertheless he was able to feed his children well and led a luxurious life. Even during his exile he was able to build his obi and reach out himself in his mother's land. This self-confidence and the serfdom was completely washed away by the white man's religion. Though the forefathers of Isaac Okonkwo followed the system of polygamy, none of them desolated their wives and children. Christianity proclaims itself as the religion of the living God but it levies taxes in order to proclaim the word of god, But in *Arrow of God* Ezeulu though he worshipped the unknown god or the spirits or idols lived a luxurious life. Isaac having accepted Christianity is well known that polygamy is a sin, and so he has one wife. But he struggles hard to fulfil the needs of his children and the family. The entanglement of the native religion and Christianity is felt in every bit of the behavior of Obi. He is not against Christianity and not against his religion as well.

Achebe has tremendously sculpted the character of Obi as a mere representative of the post-colonial situation. Obi likes to hear folk songs from his mother, but his mother is frightened to sing because his father considers it as a heathen practice. Obi's father said " We are not heathens,' stories like that are not for the people of the church" (NLE, 46). Achebe discusses how the white man had such power over the native people. The Christian Missions were the first to set up printing presses in the land. For the first time, people were able to find something in the written form. In *Arrow of God* Achebe states that "Mr Okonkwo believed utterly and completely in the things of the white man. And the symbol of the white man's power was the written word, or better still, the printed word" (NLE, 100). Okonkwo feels overwhelmed by the power that white man has: According to him the written word is the Uli that never faded as forecasted by his ancestors. He also illustrates that the books written many years ago remain the same and nothing can be changed. Okonkwo gives reference to the written word as referred to by Pilate in The Bible. “What is written is written” (NLE, 101). Okonkwo’s admiration towards the printing press and the written word can be identified from his room which is filled up with many types of written materials ranging from 1908 to 1920. His place was fully occupied with books everywhere. It is very much evident that Okonkwo was completely under the rule of Whiteman’s thoughts and actions unlike his father who stood alone against the white man and committed suicide unable to withstand the cowardice of his own people.

Christianity has brought many changes among the natives, that they were able to forget even the age old practices. For instance, Osu is the name given to those people who are dedicated to Gods and they are considered as outcasts and are not allowed to marry any other people of the land. Achebe tries to break the ignorance of the native people through the character of Obi. After Obi came to know Clara is an Osu he does not hesitate to get married to her. He believes that his father will not be against it because his father is now a long way from the practices and customs of his land. The religious, traditional and cultural devastation that is caused due to the white man’s religion is deduced from the conversation of Obi and his father. The native people suffered the trauma of adapting themselves completely to the new religion. As said the African Christians accepted what they wanted and kept aside some memorable practices of their forefathers just as the belief in the outcast. Roger that “Achebe wishes to present Obi Okonkwo above all as a man of words as evident in his treatment of the major crises of Obi’s childhood, all of which relate to the world of "book" and suggest that European education and values constitute the germ of his later alienation and betrayal of his parents’ world”(166).

The Missionaries cannot perform individually in the non-western countries and so they ordained clergy men as well as the catechist. In *No Longer at Ease* Isaac Okonkwo was a catechist and had served in the church for nearly thirty years. Mission school served the purpose of the missionaries. The missionaries, by opening the schools, were not only able to civilize the natives but also were able to deliver them the doctrine of Christianity. Cox says "Education was not to be a consolation prize, but a key engine of Christianization" (162).

Achebe is particular in painting the aesthetic beauty of the Igbo society with a slight sense of humor. Achebe portrays the loss of tradition and the hold of the government through a situation. When Obi's father was working as a Catechist in Aninta, the he-goat of the great gods Udo created great menace in the church and ate all the yams and the maize crops. Once it ate all the yams cooked by Mrs. Okonkwo who raged with anger and cut the head of the goat. Initially this created hatred among the village elders, and she was refused to sell as well as buy from the market. "But so successful had been the emasculation of the clan by the white man's religion and government that the matter soon died" (NLE, 133). "As the hero of Achebe's story, Obi reveals how the use of cultural assimilation of colonial Nigeria contradicts to a large extent the aim of its outspoken defenders in the circle of Christian missionaries and educators. He admits like Achebe himself the gross error of Europeans in Africa" (Babolala, 140).

Obi transforms into a realist, and he wants to get rid of the illusion that the white government and his education has brought to him. He knows that he was seduced by the culture and the city of Lagos. Though being educated in the CMS School and having learnt the values of the

Christian he was one among the Nigerians who were lost in the entanglement of religion, culture and civilization. Osu was a taboo in his tradition and the same Osu or outcasts were accepted in the church. It is this concept of tumult, which Obi is not able to overcome as a Christian convert. He fumbled with Colonial ideas, and he adhered to the principles of the white man's religion, but the Nigerian in him terminated his vision for the future. Achebe in *No Longer at Ease* tries to bring the cultural limbo of the natives that leads them to devastation. Unlike the heroes of Achebe's previous novel, Obi is not relentless. He is a young man crippled by the culture of the city of Lagos. He could neither forfeit his tradition nor his enjoyments offered by his position in the city of Lagos. Babolala is clear about "Achebe's satire that Obi Okonkwo, with his education and insight into modern life, may never attempt to alter his complex personality and the image of a colonial society in which he lives among others" (87).

Pandurang quotes some lines from Petals of Blood to exemplify the effect of Christianity over the Igbo society. It says "The Missionary carried The Bible, the soldier carried the gun, the administrator and the settler carried the coin. Christ, commerce, civilization, The Bible, the coin, the gun" (16). The Post colonial era proved the religious practices of the Igbo people false and made the path easier for the converts. The evangelists were very clear in the mission towards the African country. They fought against paganism and proved that idol worship is a disgrace and they negated all the practices of the Igbo tradition. As Blake observes "Values that Africans revered and invoked during ceremonial occasions were denigrated by the colonial powers, rendering practices informed by African values as "barbaric" or "devilish" (86).

The foremost idea of the mission was to colonize. The Mission preached to the people that they were worshipping dead gods and they are conducted to any type of danger .The missionaries also threatened that all their practices were something occult and they in their lifetime should live horrified. "Belief in ancestral spirits is sheer nonsense and hogwash," (Blake, 86). Thus these ideas were inculcated in the minds of the native people .One such idea is treating an Osu as a normal human being. It is this idea that forces Obi Okonkwo to dispute with his father about his marriage with Clara. Obi's father a staunch Christian believes that marrying an Osu will surely bring disgrace to the family. So he strictly warns Obi that he cannot marry an Osu. Obi's 1 father said "Osu is like leprosy in the mind of our people" (NLE, 106). The destruction of the native practices is brought in the argument of Obi with his father. Obi asked his father "What made an Osu different from other men and women? Nothing but the ignorance of their forefathers. Why should they, who had seen the light of the Gospel, remain in that ignorance"? (107). Obi is not a rigid convert but he is a perfect epitome of the disintegrated youth of the past colonial era. Unlike his father Okonkwo, Isaac Okonkwo is entrapped between the two customs and beliefs though he wanted to remain a true Christian, and this stops him from accepting an Osu as his daughter in-law. Mezu Rose observes: "Despite his ambivalence and his firm Christian beliefs, on the issue of the Osu system which defines not self- image but self-identity, Isaac Nwoye Okonkwo will not budge" (74).

Umuofia at the outset of colonization was proud of the past and the country was jeweled with the beliefs of the past, its tradition, rituals, ceremonies and the ancestors which were demolished by the arrival of Christianity. It alienated the people from their cherished practices which were considered as the treasure of the country. We have come across the term Osu from the first novel of Achebe, but in *No Longer at Ease* the emphasis is laid on the protagonist's transformation. Achebe has beautifully captured a situation to lay stress upon the abolition of the customary practice of not marrying an Osu, wherein he entwined romance with the serious issue. Thereby the serious tone of the native custom is understood in its entire vibes. The African continent and its inhabitants have suffered a great deal of aggression on their characters. Blake is rather critical when he states that the 'barbarous', the 'dark' and the 'uncivilized' had to be civilized.

The outsiders, mainly the Europeans, conquered the country through various instruments

in different junctures. Blake states two instruments through which the outsiders got into contact with the Africans. Initially it was the trans –Atlantic slave trade and secondly colonialism which they used to transform the so called barbarous African. Evangelization was a part of colonization which affected the larger part of the community and later on it helped the Europeans in the height of colonization. The evangelists bombarded the core or the root of the customs, the 'heathenism' which is the base of African culture. Achebe has wrought these changes in his first three novels. As per Oliver States that "Cultures differ, and minds, feelings and intentions in differing societies intermesh in differing ways" (Blake, 27).

Achebe has crafted the characters which undergo the process of civilization through means of religion, education, status, and the culmination of the culture. Obi as an individual is the internal force through which the external force of colonization works. The change that

Oliver refers to intercedes in the entire situation in the story of *No Longer at Ease*. The youth of the colonized era have lost track and they are very much imbibed with the culture and ideas of the colonizers. The passage of colonization was through Christianity. The hero of the novel Obi Okonkwo transforms himself into a colonized youth and he is carried away by the flashes of the city of Lagos. Initially the Church transformed the religious practices, and then it laid principles for an individual to follow and ultimately the religion remodeled the character of the individual. Obi Okonkwo is the result of an individual's mutation caused by colonization.

Achebe wrought the character of Obi in such a way it embodies every facet of the colonized era. Obi's urge to marry an Osu emerges from the belief of Christianity wherein the religion preaches all are equal in the sight of god. Obi convinces his father who resisted: "But all that is going to change. In ten years things will be quite different to what they are now" (NLE, 107).Achebe has forecasted the future of the nation through the words of Obi Okonkwo. "Christianity, its religion, is deeply entrenched in several African countries and has denigrated and replaced indigenous religions and belief systems, and in the process, negatively affected whatever is left of her civilization" (Blake, 67).

The post-colonial era was a plethora of demoralizations. The native youngsters were lost in the flood of excitement entangled with the beliefs of the new religion. Though they were Africans all their attitudes were colonized. Such was the situation in *No Longer at Ease*. The moral destruction of the youngsters of the post-colonial era begins in *No Longer at Ease* as they travel the demoralized behavior of getting bribes. It was their initial act towards destruction. Later on it turned into politics. As Roger states "Obi's experience in *No Longer at Ease* reveals the implications of this double meaning: the word of white power also portends black spiritual decay and death" (166).

The colonization was the curbing of the black by the white. In the period of Obi's grandfather in spite of their illiteracy every action and behavior of the Africans emerged so as to develop the clan and themselves. However, it was not only Christianity that brought changes in the native character of the Igbo, even many years back slavery trade brought a great change in the form and behavior of the native people. Africa formed the major part of the slavery trade and it was said that Africa was important for two slavery trade, the black ivory and the other is white ivory. "Christianity could no longer be represented as a force extraneous to the African experience but a crucial part of the social and cultural fabric of postcolonial society" (Gikandi, 155).

The religion which has been the major area for transforming has taken extreme flight in the novels of Chinua Achebe. It is in *Things Fall Apart* that the disintegration begins and ultimately flourishes effectively in the last trilogy *No Longer at Ease*. Achebe has been a victim in the crossroads of culture affected by Christianity and has experienced the damage done by the religion. In *Man of the People* Christianity has taken complete control over the country, and to the people of Ananta, Christmas has become their religious celebration in the place of the New Yam festival. Most of the religious concepts of the Igbo tradition are totally forgotten. The Christian population that has gathered in the Ananta too seems to be extravagant, "Its sons and daughters who have gone out to work or trade in the cities usually return home with lots of money to spend" (MOP, 87). The white man's religion has brought a sophisticated life to the people and they have been transformed totally .Odili Samalu talks about the transformation: "The boys I saw that morning wore Italian –type shoes and tight trousers and the girls wore lipstick and hair stretched with hot iron; I even saw one in slacks, which I thought was very bold indeed" (MOP, 87).

People chose Christianity not for salvation but for its glamour and the opportunities it provided like education, trade, etc. Chief Nanga is a disintegrated man, who has sold himself for the religion considering himself civilized and cultured after he followed this white man's religion but in vain. To secure his position he behaves like a Christian and follows his ways, but he forgets that The Bible says that "The wages of sin is death." If he has accepted the religion wholly he would not amass wealth because it is said in The Bible that it is not easy for a rich man to enter the door of heaven. The Mask dance of the ancestral spirit is replaced by the mask of Christmas father and the 'Ogene' is replaced by drums and trumpets. The seriousness of the mask dance is replaced by the comical dancing of the mask. The song:

Sunday, bigi bele
Sunday Sunday, bigi bele
Sunday Akatakata done come !
Everybody run away!
Enday, Alleluia! (MOP 88)

In *Anthills of the Savannah* "Achebe tries to think differently. History remains to Achebe as the story of a people, always ethnic. History is always the narrative of destiny" (Echerou, 67). Parry defines that "A 'post-colonial' view of history is It enables us to understand what a people process of a particular form of political and cultural an important, even 137 crucial moment in a process acknowledges that colonialism was, indeed, a fact unerasable one at that. It reminds us that her postcolonial condition can never be the 'true' colonialism and in this sense, is an age of innocence" (67). "Accordingly, Hebraic faith and Christian practice become moments to ponder in the extended history of the people of Idemili whose priestess is the novel's heroine. In that history, the Christian moment is no longer the coming of Christ, but the Westernization of the Jesus doctrine. Indeed, as the novel tells it, the transformation was not unconnected with the inventiveness of that Western institution of the monastery where European Christianity was really born" (Echeruo, 72). "Christianity and traditional Igbo religion seemingly differ only in form, but not in essence. Dogmas of both religions underwent changes that improved the position of women, elevating them from their lowly position to a pedestal where they could remain admired, but inconsequential" (Mitrovic, 41). In other words colonialism drives the history of a nation towards a lot of vicissitudes and moreover the transformation that happens to the society, its people and its culture is unrepairable.Achebe's novels exemplify the drastic changes that colonization brought over the Igbo tradition.

The Igbo society underwent a lot of crisis with the intrusion of colonial rule. The womb of Igbo tradition was aborted by the impact of the white colonial rule. Africa had a lot of intruders in the previous centuries but they were affected only by slave trade and plundering of the foreigners. But the arrival of Europeans totally changed the structure of the Continent itself. Though Samuel Ikedi had become a Christian, he sticks on to the values of Igbo tradition. He is against getting married to White women. "The tussles between African legal systems and colonial law, in Achebe's fiction, serve as a framing device for the ongoing changes in the constitution of social imaginaries since changes in law create new moral orders and ways of apprehending dissatisfaction with the imagination of the collective"(Osinubi, 30).

The missionaries opened many schools in all the remote parts of the village. They proved all the superstitious beliefs wrong and then initiated a trust in the mind of the people, giving a hope of the deliverance from darkness. Achebe shows in his novels how the age-old practices were demolished by Christianity, through which the religion got many converts. For example, the evil forest, the twin babies, the outcasts were encouraged in the church. This created curiosity among the Igbo and they joined the religion just like others without a purpose behind. The white man along with his religion has brought forth his government to control the barbaric quality of the people.

Christianity supported and was moreover the stepping stone towards the success of the colonial power. Any power cannot be sustained just by transforming an individual of a society. Instead the values, its culture and its tradition should be completely rooted out.Colonizers believed very much in destroying the very root of the Igbo tradition, so that their place and their purpose would remain intact. Christianity and its power in breaking the communal rites are depicted in the novels of Chinua Achebe.

References :

Chinua, Achebe. *A Man of the People.* London: Penguin Classics, 2001.Print.

.... *Anthills of the Savannah.* London: Penguin Classics, 2010.Print

.... *Arrow of God.* London: Penguin Classics, 2010.Print

.... Achebe, Chinua. *Things Fall Apart*. London: Penguin Classics, 2001.Print

Blake, Cecil. *The African Origin of Rhetoric*: New York, London: Routledge, Taylor and Francis group, 2009.N List Web December 1 2016.

Cox, Jeffery. The British Missionary Enterprise since 1700: New York, London:Routledge, Taylor and Francis group, 2009. N List. Web November 15 2016.

Giovannucci, Peri. *Literature and development in North Africa: The Modernizing Mission*.New York, London: Routledge, Taylor and Francis group, 2008.N List Web 21 December 2016.

Granqvist, Raoul. "The Early Swedish Reviews of Chinua Achebe's "*Things Fall Apart*" and "A *Man of the People*". *Research in African Literatures*, Vol. 15,No. 3.1984:394-404 Indiana University Press. N. List. Web. December 1 2016.

Killam, G. D. "Chinua Achebe's Novels." *The Sewanee Review*, Vol. 79, No. 4 197:514 – 541. The Johns Hopkins University Press *N. List*. Web .December 1 2016.

Loomba, Ania. Colonialism/ Post colonialism, 2nd edition: New York: Routledge,Taylor and Francis Group, 2005.N list Web November 15 2016.

Mercedes, Mackay. "*Arrow of God* by Chinua Achebe." *African Affairs*, Vol. 63,No. 253 1964:303-304. Oxford University Press on behalf of The RoyalAfrican Society. *N. List*. Web December 1 2016.

Okuma, Peter Chidi. Dieux, Hommes et Religions: Towards an African Theology:The Igbo context in Nigeria. Bruxelles, BE: Peter Lang AG, 2002. ProQuest ebrary. Web. 9 November 2016.

Osinu bi, Taiwo Adetun j. "Chinua Achebe and the Uptakes of African Slaveries."Research in African literatures, V.40, No. 4 (2009): 1-23.N List Web Nd.

Pandurang, Mala. *Chinua Achebe: An Anthology of Recent Criticism*. Delhi. Pencraft International. 2010. Print

Podis, Leonard A, Yakubu Saaka. “Anthills of the Savannah and Petals of Blood: The Creation of a Usable Past.” *Journal of Black Studies,* V.22, No. 1, *African Aesthetics in Nigeria and the Diaspora* (1991):104-122. Sage Publications, Inc. *N List*, Web December1 2016.

Povey, John. “Anthills of the Savannah by Chinua Achebe.” *African Arts*, Vol. 21,No. 4 1988: 21-23. UCLA James S. Coleman African Studies Center. *N List.*Web December 1 2016.

Rhoads, Diana Akers Culture in Chinua Achebe’s Things Fall Apart. *African StudiesReview*, Vol. 36, No. 2 1993:61-72. Cambridge University Press. *N. List*. Web December 1 2016.

Rose, Mezu. Chinua Achebe: The Man and His Works. London: Adonis & Abbey Publishers Ltd.2006. ProQuest ebrary. Web. 9 November 2016.

Searle, Alison. “The Role of Missions in Things Fall Apart and Nervous Conditions.”Literature & Theology, Vol .21. No.1. 2007.49-65. Advance Access publication.N. List. Web. November 12, 2016.

Soile, Sola. “Tragic Paradox in Achebe’s Arrow of God.” Phylon (1960), Vol. 37,No.3.1976:283-295.Clark Atlanta University. N. List. Web. December 1 2016.

Ward, Abigail. “Psychological Formulations”. The Routledge Companion to Postcolonial

Studies. Ed. John McLeod: London New York: Routledge, Taylor and Francis

group, 2007. N. List. Web December 18 2016.

www.ingramcontent.com/pod-product-compliance
Ingram Content Group UK Ltd.
Pitfield, Milton Keynes, MK11 3LW, UK
UKHW042001190726
13854UKWH00005B/2097

9 798885 305013